Rough Traces

Jason Wesco

Shake Dust Press – Damascus, Nebraska

First Paperback Edition. First Printing

Library of Congress Control Number: 2007926811

ISBN: 0-9740159-9-7

Designed by Christine Ewing

Manufactured in the U.S.A.

Shake Dust Press
Damascus, NE

For O. P. G.

May your tap be open when it rusts.

Every man's life ends the same way and it is only the details of how he lived and how he died that distinguishes one man from another.

Ernest Hemingway

Contents

Notes

Acknowledgements

Thanks

The Author

1

Having Weather

The Flea Market in White Cloud

We shared an elephant ear. It made you
think of Oklahoma (even though that was
an elephant's eye). You sang a little. I
remember thinking how much I hated
that song until I heard you sing it.

I bought a can of roach killer (circa 1939)
and a Jughead hat that you insisted on
wearing the rest of the day. You didn't
buy anything. Nothing tickled you, you
said. And I laughed. You poked my ribs
and asked. So I told you about a coach
that used to say *if I had your talent and
you had a feather up your ass, we'd both
be tickled.* Root beer came out of your nose.

I tried on a snorkel mask, a pair of flippers
and a yellow flotation device that looked
like a duck. I said I'd always wanted to
wear something like that to my neighbor's
annual Marshmallow and Weiner Roastin'
Fandango. Jim lives in a trailer, see, and has
this little plastic pool. Wouldn't that be a hoot.

Then you lifted up the mask and said *wear
that get up to my place sometime and see
what happens. I don't have a plastic pool,
but I do have a little pink claw foot tub.
It's so small that once you get in, you won't
even have room to change your mind.*

For four dollars all this can be yours.

I considered the offer and handed the man a five.

She Says Timothy

This isn't the day
for this she says.
We're having weather
with more on
the way. She snaps

beans over
the sink and
remembers certain things
on the line. A stiff

breeze snaps those
things, popping
like her beans. She
brings them in a
little wet. And another

popping; the vein
in her neck. So now
I know, but it took
time to learn.

Apple Jack is what
she wants. So, I pour
a little and she goes

back to her beans. I sit
on a metal chair and
lean, whittling nothing
into nothing. She says Frank

what's this for. And I say
nothing, sweet. She has
another drink and dries
her hands with her eyes

out the window. Says
sometimes when I sleep
I dream I'm a bicycle
tire in the rain. All treads
and spinning. Throwing
the little beads away.

I step behind her and
say something soft.
Walk her to the guest
room and help her out

of her apron. She lies
on her side and closes
her eyes. I say easy and

sleep and picture this
bed in a field of
rye, maybe, or timothy.

The Jackfruit Tree

You say your
English is slipping,
almost

broken. That
the words
are vanishing.
That no one there
speaks

the language
and that's why
you don't

write. But if I
come, you say,
we'll walk
to the foot

of a tree
so full of
pale
fruit that I
wouldn't

believe even
if you could
explain. There, you
promise
to peel tropical
skin, to share

bared flesh.
Then, you say, maybe
your stumbling,
sticky lips will
remember

my tongue.

Salamonie

We're bouncing hard
across the rez-er-vore (how
we say it in Indiana to

make it ours) sitting on
seatbacks how its done
our faces red over the

glass as she cuts
the prop hair comes
down our backs and into
the cove we go

wakeless as a backlit man
stands gesturing a friend
that casts spinning

tackle into wind a
can in one hand and
us coming in behind
when the other's hands go

quiet and fisted into his
hips he leans back
slightly sort of
proud as we pass close

enough to notice
a comfortable grin
and unlocking his
stance still

pissing makes
the air familiar
as his Ranger teeters
with the waves

West of Key West

Waymore says the sailing he had off the - what islands
were they - on a catamaran was the best in
recollection.

Fort Jefferson and the Noddy Terns,
the reef and turtles
and this miss from a crab shack in the Keys.
The one with the key lime pie.

The one that made the tongue buzz. They snorkled.
Drank tequila and Cointreau from a canteen
and smoked Fuentes, lit from cedar,
him and this waitress.

It was spring. The varied birds were moving through.

He'd never seen water that way. Weekends they
camped on islands. Places that would make him
swear by pirates and sunken treasure.

This was before he dispatched for Commercial
Freight.

And those islands, pretty as they were, had a rough
Cuban name.

If the trailer ever catches, try for this picture here,
he says.
Her name was Carmen.

His mind rests on her every now and again. Her skin
against those sand islands
on that catamaran
off Garden Key
in the Dry Tortugas.

That's how they were known, he says.
The Dry Tortugas.

It meant turtle in her tongue.

II

A Highway
Outside Poughkeepsie

Deliliah Shopteese and Her Pug Ruckus

walk past Cecil
and me eating a box
of chocolates shaped
like shoes and Cecil,

Cecil Hanratty, says
she gives off something
he ain't smelt since
God himself was in
knee pants and whistling.

That it's been a long
time since, a long time
and lilac, by Christ,
hoss, that's it. Like his
old lady wore some years
back before she went

cold fish. That he'd even
be good to that miserable
mistake for a mush runt
mutt for one more go

between a pair of
shoes like that. Yes,
sir. All the kibble he
could muster for just
a little bit. He rubs

his bald head and spits.
But what could his
tired ass do to please
a dame as fine as Delilah.
Or any damn dame at that.

Cecil says by Christ,
hoss, if it don't go
south on a fella before
he knows. Like shootin'
pool with a rope.

Revival Antiques

There's a glass bird on a coffee table that's wearing
a green top hat and dipping it's snout in a squat
glass. But the water doesn't go down. The bird
has a red ass. Beside this bird are three metal
monkeys. One is plugging his ears. Another
is peeking through his fingers. The last is covering
his mouth. Next to them, a ceramic man sits under
a tree. He looks up to a bird with its tail raised.
The inscription says *Go ahead, everyone else does.*

Then there's a wooden box. The label has a
woman with a fan. It says *Corina Larks. Extra
Mild. 15C.* And a picture of a woman in a habit
smiling through the bars of a hoosegow. And
a man riding a two story ear of corn like a horse.
A bottle of Bay Rum. A bottle of 7-UP. A badger
bristle brush. And a stag handled rusted razor.

Behind you is a pennant that roots for Wabash
College. A poster of DeNiro in *Raging Bull.*
You think of LaMotta and Salvy and Sugar Ray
in slow-motion and Jake saying *you never got
me down, Ray.* Then you flip over a Queen eight
track. You read *Another One Bites the Dust* and
Crazy Little Thing Called Love. The cover has
the band in leather. A beer stein from Baraboo
is next to a mirror in the shape of a horseshoe
that reminds you of something you already saw.

You go back for the Soviet pocketwatch with the
Kremlin on the case and the red hammer and sickle
on the face. On the way upstairs is a bookshelf
with *Das Kapital* next to *God Wants You to be Rich*
next to a book of poems by Harley Elliott next to
a pair of Groucho Marx glasses. You try them out.
Ask a man in a come-to-Jesus collar what he thinks.
He says he liked Harpo best. He points out a post-
card of hippies and tramps that reads *Hobohemia.*

You turn and pay cash. Go outside for a foot long
from the cart. Listen to the guys busk. Flip them a
few nickels. You try to imagine having nowhere to be.
Then you crack the book and sit until the light gets
thin. Straighten your leg and lean back, reaching
into your pocket. Spring the lid. Set the hands.
Wind the stem.

Sometimes I Take My Bike

When I sleep I dream
I'm late. Not for anything
I can remember. When I wake
up. I don't have anyplace
to be. Isn't that funny? It is

to me. First, I go to the post
office on fifth. It's something.
With big metal doors and lots
of echoes. I check my mail.
General Delivery. Then I look
at the posters by the door. Just
to be sure Johnny Law isn't
looking for me! I go have some
oatmeal and a Cherry Coke at
The Downtowner next. I'm there

until three. An hour past close.
Today there is a man in a hole
outside the window with a jack
hammer hammering. Three men
stand around the hole trying to
hold their maps in the wind.
I watch their mouths and make
up how they talk. Scott the bike

cop comes along and he asks
about a lady with a red wig and
a tattoo of Kansas on her leg. I
saw her at Quincy Street Station
yesterday but I don't tell. I say to
check the Mission. Then I take
the blue line (the number one, not
the other blue one) to Oakland and
watch a kid fly a kite in the park.
It's a black one with big bloodshot
eyes. I see a man walking

after rehab. He says a fiver says
I can't guess his age. He's right.
There's a man in suspenders and
shiny shoes walking a wiener dog
named Mr. B. Manny on the mower
waves me over. He asks me to paint
a hydrant like a person. A fireman,
maybe. Or a French maid. He winks
when he says that. Manny says

I'm the man and that he likes my
stuff. This is the second time this
month. Then I hop the number one,
change to the number eleven brown
bus to the number three red one (I write
this on all on my hand to remember).
The red bus driver is a new guy that
doesn't say anything when I smile.
But he does drop me at Chita's. I have
a burrito and some Pez. Jilly laughs
because it's always a different head.
Not always, but that's what she
says. Then I visit Bill the typewriter

repairman (I go backwards on my hand
to get to him). Who knew says a man
in a purple shirt that interrupts us. Bill
says fine, fine and writes a ticket. And
I say sure, sure and that I know how it
is and go next door to the rare book
store. But there's nothing worth telling

about there. Then I walk back and sit
on the porch. Well, It's a stoop, really.
There's a shovel leaning on the shed.
It's a reminder. I just leave it to lean
and drink some diet root beer. My land
lady calls me late. But she's nice mostly.
She told my mother that I was a cracker

jack something or other last time she
came. Her husband was Wilbur and he
wore a welder's mask at work and some
times even at home when they danced
because he said the sparks in her smile
were as bright as any arc weld flash.
Goddamn. And when he died, she gave
me his mask. And I guess I lied. I do
have places to be and sometimes I take
my bike.

For a Few Decks of Luckies

Tommy Mechalo, 1106 the Paseo, left
home one Thursday in August, 1929,
with his coat and hat for gas and oil.
He took along his Boston Terrier, Boyo.
When he didn't return by Friday, his wife
called the sheriff (knowing his record of
21 arrests since 1920 for investigation in
connection with crimes from tire theft to
murder) to see if Tommy was in jail.
For once, no, said Deputy Jones and so
she went looking along Forest Ave. near
Independence Boulevard where her daddy-o
had been known to go to get blotto. She
found his Hudson (with the big six) skidded
into the curb. Inside was his hat and coat
and Boyo. Two cars with men on the running
boards were seen speeding away about
eleven o'clock the night prior said a neighbor.

Mrs. Mechalo took a jitney to a fortune
teller, a negro, that saw in her crystals
Tommy's body lying along a lone country
road. She told the cops it was a mysterious
phone call because who would believe
a fortune teller, especially a negro. But she
believed, said Mrs. Mechalo, especially since
she and Tommy were run out of Chicago.
They came back to KC two months ago.
Don't we know said the sheriff and Jones
but maybe he's on the hooch and on a toot
or with a quiff and too itchy to come home.

It was almost a week that Lousie Jacoby
drove with her boys from Boone to a farm
five miles southeast of Overland Park near
108th and Mission Road. The first thing
the boys wanted to do was fish Indian Creek.
Grandad's dogs led them along the bank
and barked into the tall weeds. It was Tommy
Mechalo (also known in the underworld as
Hong Kong, Heavy and Chink) with seven
to the body and one to the head. His tongue
was cut loose and stuffed in his vest.

A note pinned to his chest mentioned his
loose lips and a load of opium enough
to sink three ships.

It must have been Lazia's men, said Mrs.
Mechalo. The North Enders, Gizzo, Gargotta,
Carollo, Scola, and Fascone. And she made
Johnny Lazia her problem and Jimmy "Needles"
LaCapra, Johnny's lieutenant, her man.
She worked LaCapra and waited five years
for her chance.

July, 1934. Johnny and his wife, Marie,
were returning from Lake Lotawana,
southeast of Kansas City. At about three,
the driver pulled into the Park Central Hotel
driveway. Two shadows opened on him with
a sawed-off and a Tommy. The driver sped
Marie off to safety as the two gunsels threw
lead at Johnny in the street.

Lazia's gang fingered Jimmy. And nearly
nixed him near Wichita that July, but Jimmy
Needles got free and was advised by G-men
to leave for South America where he had
family. But Jimmy scrammed east where his
bullet riddled body was found by police on
a highway outside Poughkeepsie.

Mrs. Mechalo (she never married Jimmy)
was there, not in Poughkeepsie, see, but
at the Park Central Hotel, July 10th at three
with a Winchester 21 pistol-gripped dually.
This is mostly how she explained to me
from a rocker on the porch out front of
the home across the street where there
were rules about smoking what she called
sticks that I snuck in exchange for a story
something like this.

Like a biker

He swaggers
like he isn't trying
to hide the gimp
he brought back
from an oil rig
somewhere in Texas

His face looks
like he just fell
off a raft. Wears
those boots with
wide straps, metal
rings and rivets.
Red bandana, a vest
and (no shit) chaps.

Like a biker.
But, he doesn't
have a bike.

He calls it his
get up. Like that pole
vaulter in Athens. He
doesn't know the name
or the country.

He does know one
thing, though, that
wherever whatshisnuts
is from, he speaks better
English than those, by god,
doorknobs in Texas.

Don't get him
wrong, he's no English
major. But he'll be
damned at what they
do to the language.

And so, this once,
he said as much
to a particular
string tie wearin'
tight jeanser (built,
however, like a brick one)
Well. That. And.

That he was all
hat and no cattle,

which accounts
for the leg.

The Man at the Doughnut Shop

His clothes are ruined.
The hole is more honorable
than the patch, he says.

He drinks juice.
Eats plain cakes.
Gives advice.
And reads day old papers.
He's there
at different times
on different days
on different stools.
or in a booth
with grey tape losing to rips.

He works the swing at the paper
company. Or so he says.

Sometimes he writes.
He *essays*, mostly, he says.
He defines it for me.
Tried a poem once.
But it was *just a phrase*
he was going through.

He tells me to lighten up.
Seriousity thrills the rat.
He talks like this.
Calls himself *punny*.
Asks if he ever gets my
bearded,
horned,
four-legged,
ruminant mammel.
He nudges me.
You know, your goat.

He comes in quiet once.
Sits and says nothing.
I ask (of course).

There's bad news, he says, looking down.

(a long pause)

The Martians have landed.

(another pause)

The good news
is that
they eat Republicans
and pee gasoline.

He crosses his arms.
Sits back.
Proud enough for both of us.

Gorgeous George's Used Hat Emporium

he's been fitting faces
for sixty-five years
knows the brim, the rise
the crown for the slender
man, the squat man,
the man with a receding
chin, and the man with prominent ears.
can guess your
size to an eighth.
knows
the size of men he fit
in his father's store.
Caruso, seven and a half.
LaGuardia, the same.
Hoover, the bastard, also seven and a half.
F.D.R., seven and three-eighths.
can explain why hatters went mad
with the Danbury Shakes.
but enough about that,
he says, grabbing my arm,
let's see what we've got.
a straw Bogart.
a straw Boater.
a Fedora with a red feather.
a fur lined Bowler.
a Panama Gambler.
a wide brimmed Plantar.
a Newsboy, maybe
or
a black Porkpie
with New York felt
a black band
one and one-quarter inch
stingy brim
and a
tear
drop
crown.
seven and three-eighths, he guesses
pressing it down.
looks in the mirror.
steps away, says
sharp, son, sharp
as a straight razor shave

III

Some Maps of Kansas

Valley Falls

I'm thumbing
through old
photos and come to
a group of cigar
factory men.
Sleeves rolled.
Rough chinned.
Sloppy.
Tough.
They look up.
None smile.
Just look.

Around them
are presses,
shears,
a spittoon,
leaves
and molds.
On the wall
behind, a leg angles
the page above
the days of May.

The men draw
my eyes away.
But then, again
the leg
becomes all I see.

Small there,
over his shoulder.
Nearly a century
away.

Perry

I remember. Kunkle ran
the ferry. Three cents for
a man, five for a hog. Rising
Sun wasn't yet under the plow.
I heard ladies there were kind
in their ways. Our place was
up in the bluffs, mostly pasture.
Three veins of hardwood and
rolling slopes. A nice treed draw.
We ran fifty head. And shoed
horses some, too. Town had
a common well, a band, an opera
house, two hotels and an African
Baptist Church off Second. The
Presbyterians were there and
Methodists. A milliner and cobbler.
The Plug made runs through to
Topeka and Lawrence. Stopped
off at Grantville and Williamstown.
Mail came thrown from the train.
They grew potatoes in the Half-
Breed Lands between the tracks and
the Kaw. Shipped them out on U.P.
freights. Folks from Valley Falls
boated down the Delaware once
for the July 4th picnic. Eddie
Rickard was my best friend.
Stark was mayor.

Kentucky Bottoms

Name the town. Give
it a river. Or two
that bend

together. And tracks
the length of it,
busy from

trains. Streets with trees
all out of leaves.
Sheds down

alleys that lean. A few
sidewalks cracked
open with

weeds. Porches with
paint bent in peels.
Some strays

getting familiar over
a stopped sewer
grate.

A lady with a limp
clipping wash
on the line.

Two men in suspenders
blowing smoke at
each other.

Add an elevator, rusted,
and emptied
of grain.

Work in some pigeons
to dot roofs
and fences.

Finish with
weather.

The Facts of a Place

There are seventeen hundred miles
of road in Ellis County.

German iron crosses in the grave
yard at Saint Fidelis.

Ninety-six stone bridges.

Thirteen plaques that commemorate
historic structures. Nine for
saloons, gambling houses and brothels.

Annual precipitation of 21.85 inches.

740 farms on 565,000 acres.

Fifteen towns: Antonio, Ellis and Emmeram,
Hays, Hog Back, Midian and Munjor,
Pfeifer, Schoenchen, Toulon and Turkville,
Victoria and Walker and Yocemento.

Rohr Jacobs Lake, Wildon Draw,
Big Creek and the Smoky Hill River.

A woman that can recite the Gettysburg
Address in sixty seconds.

The Lamer Hotel where Hemingway slept.

Streets once policed by Hickock, Masterson and
Earp.

Campaign stops by J.F.K, T.R. and William Jennings
Bryan.

27,060 residents, approximately, some of which
who have dined at Al's Chickenette on Eighth
and Vine.

And a stranger in the library that's lost
track of time.

The Same Cafe

"The weather went and turned
off cold."

> "Prices the way they are it's a wonder
> more fellers don't
> turn to dope."

"Old Booker, his back
leg went and I had to put a slug
in his ear. Head like a mill
stone. It took twice."

> "How about a number five and a Jersey
> Highball."

"My salamander is on the blink."

> "That sorry hand
> of mine. I have half a mind to go up
> side his head with a piss elm club."

"Them two. Hotter than pepper sprouts."

> "The juice just ain't worth
> the squeeze no more, Alice, dammit."

"A pig, he gets fed. And a hog,
why a hog,
he gets slaughtered."

> "Well, Jimmy,
> I can't make
> chicken salad
> outta' chicken shit."

"Losin' a woman
fine as Faye
could make a man
sorry
to see
the sun."

> "That guy there."
> "There?"
> "No. There."
> "The one that all
> the time jots?"
> "He don't eat no pig."

"Where's Faye, Frank?"
"Her new address is Memorial Acres."
"No. I wasn't gone that long"
"It don't take long."

　　　"Last week, though, she
　　　was hotter than the hinges
　　　of Hades."

Keats

Driving past the sign
reminds me of
a poem

by a man I've never
met about a
man I

don't care to know
whether
really ever existed.
Meaning not

that I hope he didn't
only
that the truth
in
a poem is

incidental
and when known
tends to lessen
both

the truth
and the poem.

As opposed
to the truth
of
a poem
or a man
or a town

left off
some maps
of
Kansas.

Letter from Muscotah

My community is
bare. It has a non-

working gas station
and pop machines
that sell out

every week and
they don't give you

your money back.
There are a lot
of farmers that live

in old farm houses
that have red
barns in there yards.

There are pastures
and fields of all
kinds. It has a

school and its haunted
or that's what people
say, and there is a river

that goes through
the edge of town.

||||

Long Past Gone

One Man's Junk

Sixty some years
measured in screen doors,
sinks and push mowers
piled high
in the backyard.

There's a pump
from the well of his
father's farm. The '67
Datsun pickup he refers
to as the "relic." The
box of lighted rubber
balls he bought at the
auction for a quarter
after a haggle.

He makes his way
through the maze
each day revealing some
forgotten thing
to turn around
in his mind. Hold up
to the light. Inspect
with a narrowed eye.

Curator of his own
collection of memories
made real. His mind
given shape by things
being reclaimed
by rust and rot.

Returning to earth
the pieces of him.

For Some Years the Janitor at Lowman

My old man wasn't much of one.
Made most of his with a mop
and bucket up to the school
where I went.

When kids asked
I said Nah

because he stuttered
when he talked

because his left arm was gimp

because when Heather Linder
puked, my old man cleaned it
up on his knees

because his desk was by
the boiler

because he was the only man
there didn't wear a tie

because he packed his own lunch
and ate in the gym with us

because he always brought Dinty
Moore in a thermos and two
biscuits

because his truck had no air and
made jerks in low gear

because where he picked
to live

because when it came up what he did
for work, my old man never
lowered his eyes.

Muscadine

The wife, she ain't fond
of my drinkin',
so I keep a stash
in a mess
of dead timbers
along the draw.

Have me a nip of
that homemade every
now and again.

My people back
in Caroline
send it
secret
and regular.

Make it from
fruit that comes wild
on a vine
that grows
along the Scuppernong.

She's sweet as
dew,
you'll see.

Let's have us that walk.

I like to say that
everyman, on his
birthday,
having earned it,
ought to partake
in full measure,

ought to be
drunk
as he is old.

Grissom A.F.B.

They got a bead on us, them
Russkies, ya' know.
Yes, sir.
An ICBM's got our name
written all over her
painted pretty in bright red
lipstick and she's just waitin'
to give us a kiss.
Bet your sweet ass on that.

Them Air Force boys ain't
gonna' wait around for that
smooch, though.
No, sir.
Them fly boys 'll take wing
and be
long past gone
when that particular shit
hits this particular fan.

That'll leave nuthin'
but a big ole bullseye,
empty hangars
and us
if we're left, I guess.

They say around here
there'll be nuthin' left,
nuthin' but dust,
which is somethin'
that gives me comfort
in a kinda' crooked
sorta' way.

Hell, it might be a damn
site better
except for them who
gotta' sweep up
what's left
of what's not.

Terminal

The only thing that keeps me away
she says
are the appointments at the V.A.
Otherwise I'm here – most days.
She tells me that she dresses for
Sunday and looks so very forward
to this. How she knows the nice
folks that work here.
It's a small place, you know.
Mr. Jackson at the ticket counter
and the cleaning help.
Magdalena made cookies
after one of her spells.

Tells me how she waits
at the gate - all smiles - for arrivals.
Everyone needs more of those.
That sometimes she cries at departures
to show others it's okay.
It helps keep her mind off other concerns
until everyone is gone, anyway.
Then it's an awful empty quiet.
She guesses like a big house
after the holidays.

Says she'll see me off if I like.
Opens her bag and asks me
to choose a handkerchief
for her to wave.
Pats my hand.
Tells me to do the same.

Roscoe Fearing Falters

The last time I saw Roscoe Fearing Falters he was crossing
the trestle bridge over Bloodshot Creek and that damned
tricky ravine. It was August nineteen hundred seventy
something. He was in his usual blue suit and pink painter's
cap and was drinking a bottle of Sunkist (which I
remember because he never did).

Nonchalant. Roscoe used that word a lot. It described his
walk. The amble of a man looking to be surprised was the
best way I heard it put. He also liked avuncular and skinny
ties from back in the fifties.

He called me a card and his favorite shoes were stolen
from Cannonball Lanes. Red on the outside. Grey on the
in. They found a green Gideon's New Testament in his
inside pocket, but never him.

And a brothel token from Swede's good for a Whisky,
Stogie and Screw and a matchbook that promised social
advancement for the price of their pamphlet. I was next
of kin as far as could be told.

And got all this in a duffle that wasn't his. And a memo
taking him off the Riley account. It was the Chicago, Rock
Island & Pacific. I can still see those 11's on his heels in my
head walking away. It's something I can't get out.

The sun was a mean bastard that day. And Roscoe
Fearing Falters had music for a name.

~~IIII~~ I

steep Iron

Graveyard Shift

you step through
a stretch
of lamp posts met
with rails
that slant steep
iron over
stone steps tricking
up to a gate
cheated open by the
man who
says he gets
lonely for bones
as dirt comes
thrown from his
shovel glinting
moon-mad with light.

The Smithy

a hammer
is fisted
bellows lunged
tongs
neared
at the pivot
coal embers sunned
red metal struck
turned
and plunged
to hold the curve
along which
an eye
is run
by the smithy
the son
that turns out
shoes
for horsemen
that makes pig iron
wrought

city-broke

He reckons her for city-broke
on how she stands
tied and withered in the street

Says he knows the reins first-hand
drove deliveries in Chicago and
he reckons her for city-broke

The gait, the crop
how paced steps stopped
tied and withered in the street

Sure before the cart, he says
and shying from the driver's hands
He reckons her for city-broke

Beaten, brittle, tried,
spent to bones,
tied and withered in the street

Waiting for the lash, then
pulling true to task
He reckons her for city-broke
Tied and withered in the street

Kingdom Farm

The pocked blade makes
its slice. The deep
chest of his horse
heaves breath into
the sun (just up)

and strains against
the heft. The hard
ground of the lost
crop is broken back
to clods. As the
vision of Hoade
and the Twelve

Elect also was turned
back. No Christ
opened this sky. No
matter their songs
or rightly lives. How
they waited past his

death. Good years
past. And how some
thought Hoade himself
would come back

a Christ. Seasons turned
on the devout
that left. The Twelve
Elect went down

to One. One that pauses
in his plowing. One
that in Hoade's voice
still hears his hard

name ringing. One that
worked the ground
daily in wait. One
that resumes the row
that turns the last
of Kingdom Farm

under. One that unhitches
the plow, left
lodged, and walks off
with the horse from
ten years of
himself like grist
left in the mill

ground down.
Past the last hedge
post they become
dust as the red road
rises up.

The Lamplighter

puts the thick
of his
wrist
to the axe-handled
cart

he cobbled from
scrap to
make bid
for the route

that
skitters the pitched
paving
to the corner
lamp

gone coldly
out

his lungs clench
his jaw sets
his
short
smoke juts
red

against
the weather

under
the dark
lip
of his cap

In Granite and Marble

I made prayers of rock.
With a chisel I leaned over
the bench and learned:
What could be afforded the dead;
What the living demand;
What stone exacts.

The scale of a number and the kern
of a letter came to matter.
In time, my eye could match a square.
My hands became just as sure.
I knew what I'd see after blowing
a stone clean.
I'd sink a finger to clear the grooves
of grit and sweat.

I worked past my lamp.
Slept at the bench.
Didn't dream but for Ruby Blake.
What of that, I think.
I still know just where she lays.

When I walk the stone rows,
I see what I've become.
And what I was.
Since '45 each has carried my mark.
There in the corner.
Double J's on a scroll.
It's how I can be known.
Even more so than by this last one.
The letters are familiar.
But the date.
The date is tricky.

Leech & Sons

The river roils into the mill
race. Along the
flume, water
works to the wheel
that turns
wooden gears
whirring
augers
tackle
cogs
rolling stones
grinding along two
run of buhrs
on through to
the sifter,
the elevator
to sacks stacked
square on the dust
thick floors.
Thicker since
the ward
came down
with the miller's cough
that's kept him
away *too long,*
 too long says old
man Leech that dresses
and trues the stone
nights, so days
the boys
can grind fine
grist
in his mill.

For Science (and a few quid)

a shovel fisted
tough boots his
blade into
stiff
earth his teeth
are clenched
pickets his heart

misses some he
wears a stove
pipe and gone
fingered
gloves from
when
he drove the ice

wagon before he
got religion
and met
the preacher with
the slaunchways
grin
that convinced

him it's no matter
of god's nor sin
to remember
which section
of the bone
yard this is
seems a waste

not to for
science and a few
quid says
the preacher with
the slaunchways

grin to the tough
that leans and
bends which is
to say to you

you dig

Cheat River Coffinworks

Rain has turned
the dirt road
mud. You
wrestle axle
deep in slag
earth, spinning.
You know he'll
dock your check.
The way he'll
stand. Lean
asking if
your rooster
had a frog in
its chicken neck.
Laugh his coffee
breath. How
he'll wipe his brow.
Flick a finger
of sweat. How
you'll grit
your teeth
again and
not put
the jack plane
down.

||||| |

Making Good

Flush or Bust

She smokes
as you roll
up. It's late
and you figure
it won't hurt.

The grasshoppers
are something
else, she says,
crushing her
Winston how
she does when
there are no
customers.

You say
you'll have two
Nathan's Famous.
Hand her
three bucks. She
won't take
your money.

She's right.
And you know
she has a say.
But you don't
talk. Only
look out and
wonder how
you could not
have noticed.

There must
be hundreds. A
plague, you think.
Unless, of course,
you were
a toad, then
you'd be flush.

But you're not.

You roll
down the window,
chewing and
backing up
and listening
to tiny bones
gone bust.

You don't
wave.

You wish
you'd said
something, but
you go on

chewing and
driving slow
on gravel,
watching your
low beams
thinking

that her
shift is over,
sure
she'll beat you
home.

not too good

You still eat
with the mechanics
to show them.
You're not too
good. Line up
for chili dogs
and Fritos from
the *roach coach*.
You take their
jokes. It's your
clothes.

You ignore what
they say about
the new girl up
front. Her last
name is Lay.
They don't know
you're seeing
her. That's a good
thing. It wasn't
that long ago.
They remind you.
You know, you
say.

You've been
asked to join
the guys up
front (in the
break room with
their Diet Cokes
and paper sacks).
He said *colleagues*
when he asked.
Maybe you
said. But you
like the shop.
You like the
talk.

Johnny says you
have *potential*.
And he encourages
you. You knew
you wouldn't
miss the heat
or the shop boss.

So you agreed.
He put you in
sales.

It's not you.
The cheap tricks.
Word games.
Playing the
angle. Working
the lot. Sure
you've had
a good month
or two. But,
you're getting
soft.

You know it
when you reach
for the pink
soap, not the red.
Then smell
your hands.
For God's
sake.

You've started
smoking. Started
admiring how
it looks. You
stand out front
tipping ashes.
Sneaking side-
long glances
in the showroom
glass.

Today you turn.
You look. You
see. Your tight
buttoned shirt.
A roll of skin
you've never
noticed. A blue
bow tie pin
on your collar.
Your thin tie
snapping over
your shoulder
in the wind.
Your hair gone
wrong.

Burning and Dodging

This is the last
of that roll of black
and white.

You'd forgotten.

Of course, you'd
forgotten. It's been,
what, ten years
now? But as you
develop, it starts
coming back, that
day in Kansas City.

Neither of you slept
the night before.
How you shot all
day. Lugged
five cameras and
a back pack of film.

Here's where he
handed you his
camera. Ran
ahead and emptied
away into the cool
shadows. You were
left there with
the gear, exhausted.
Laughing at his
jungle sounds.
Trying to spot him
with your hand
against the glare.

You knelt between
the rails. Used
that old Nikon
with the telephoto
to zoom the shadows.

He wasn't there.

As you pulled back,
you began to see.
Let the camera go
dangling, noticing
the curve of the place
and how it made
you wonder which
curved first, the tracks
or the buildings.

The light was perfect.

You stood there,
straddling one rail.
Pointed and
angled a Canon
and made this
picture now emerging.

You never did
see him, until he
showed himself.
Said he was
right there all along
(though now you
can't recall exactly
where *there* was)
and that he imagined
it was a damn good shot.

He must be
in the frame
somewhere, you
guess, smirking
back. But you
still can't make
him out even as
you press your
eye tighter
to the loup.

After him. Now
that he's gone.

Neat

You grab two cold stones from the side
of the road. Drop them in a tumbler
with two fingers of Maker's Mark. It
was his trick. He said it was the only
way to keep it cold and truly neat. The
bag in your pocket is emptier than before.
He dug plums. You have another one.

You're sitting on a bench over
a couple named Krusmark. There's
a mausoleum with a creaked open
door. A statue of a boy writing his
own epitaph on a wall. A red
stone that reads *Ingalls* with a poem.

You walk to the fresh dirt. There's
a woman holding something you can't
name. She's six feet tall (you know
because you stood next to her on the
pedestal). She's not Mary or an angel.
Her face is granite, but her lips seem soft.

You jump down, and grab her leg for balance.
You crease your arm and lean against her.

And this is how it feels.
Making good.
Into the wind.
On his grave.
Making a mess of yourself.

Laughing like you know he would if it
had been you. It was your pact. Made
that night he showed up on your porch
in a bathrobe. Stirring a sour with his finger
and singing *I just dropped in to see what
condition my condition was in.* The rocks
rattling his glass. Not a drop missing
the changing shape of his mouth.

Now.

The rocks in your tumbler are dry.
A few more inches of bourbon
jostle the steel of your flask.
You look for colder stones.

$\cancel{||||}$ $||$

Rough Traces

Jack at the Jetlag

He tells me it was her bright idea
to up and move to New York.
They were watching the Olympics in '80
and she says something off-handed
about Lake Placid.
Next thing you know, they're on the road.
He's not sure why, but thinks she just liked
the sound of it. They've never discussed it.

Anyway, they're on the road. It's maybe a thirty
hour drive. The cats are crazy nervous.
Then a flat outside Wichita.
Tells me about the rest stop where
Knute Rockne's plane went down.
People cut off ears for souvenirs
he read somewhere. And was he ever sick,
strep it turned out. Caused them to stop
off for a doctor
And here he is, twenty-three years on.
Sometimes it still feels like a stopover.
But where the hell is he goin' at this age.

Ever since coming he's worked in hinges:

Plain Bearing Hinges
Ball Bearing Hinges
Stainless Steel Strap Hinges
Double Action Spring Gate Hinges
Drop Flap Hinges
Rising Butt Hinges
Loose Joint Hinges
and
Three-Eighths Offsets.

There's nothing in it in case I was
wondering. He was a salesman, see.
And she's still with him, by the way.
Was there through the strep, a car wreck
in '89, a heart attack, bypass and rehab.
Now this. Says he's beginning to wonder
if she's a damn jinx.

It's a joke, friend, he slurs past a jaggy
grin. Looks over his jangling glass.

Remember that.

A Clean Seam

Burt Galveston lays carpet.
So he says. Drives the yellow
truck, but you take the brunt.
You've got moxie. He says
things like that. He was a
rent-a-cop in Pisgah. Calls
you Jonsey or Mac. Digs
his nails with a carpet tack.
Why, you ask. Who's to say,
he asks. He eats oysters
with his fingers. And those
pickles in plastic. But doesn't
it. . . No. Like I said. When
he swings a hammer. If. Is
more like it. The smell. It's
something. He's got a girl.
Says it just like that. You
leave it. Lug the rolls. Alone.
It's fine, you say, forget it.
He always asks. Like he will.
Says Jonsey, where's the shag.
It's wrecked. It got wet. Again.
About that. Well. Um. Sorry.
You stare. His shirt. All his
shirts have Dave over the flap.
You'd ask. But. Then. You
find the ducts. Snap the chalk.
Nail the strips. Begin to roll
the pad, with a smoke, but you
don't. He asks if you are. You
shake your head and fumble
with the tape. Measure. Pull
the blade. He strikes a match.
Drops nuts in an RC. He forgot
the gun. The Makita. But do
you want some. He's holding
a spoon. You curse. Fling the
knife. Grab the tacker. You
make do. You. Go. On.

the bribe

you slip cash in.
run your tongue
the length of it.
lower your eyes
and pass it on.

the man in the
dark suit unfolds
his arms and
takes it to another
man who sees to it
that the man in the
white suit knows.

he's the one. he
asked. says don't
make him ask again
as he takes out a silk
handkerchief and
pats the beads
on his brow. he says
it surely is hot
tonight, but not like
it could be. that so
much depends on
this. on us, here
tonight.

brings his hands
down. follows his
finger, reading. paces.
stops. looks up
quiet. stares through
you. says something
you can't make out.
moves closer. reaches

for your wife beside
you. and she falls
limp into the arms
of one of the dark
suited men that have
come up behind.
then shouting and
noise. you notice
a large man hunched
over a Hammond

hanging on every
word from the man
in white, now without
his jacket and

his hands reach for
you and you figure
what the hell, it's
good theater. and
who's to say? maybe
its not such a bad
thing to grease
the palms that
turn the wheels of
salvation.

you close your
eyes and
fall back.

Stillwater

We drove six
hours
south of
somewhere
we wanted

out
of. Cut-timed it
to Johnny
down

I-35.
Arrived
to a waitress
with a lazy

eye
she didn't
bat
when we said
where we were
from and

why.
A quarter
television
spent
us to

dimes,
as we knocked
back black
coffee
and talked

out
the end of us
if we lasted
the ride.

Pennsylvania

You're seeing things.
Making notes on
a napkin. Outside
Carlisle in a Flying J
(with twelve diesel
lanes and twenty

-two shower stalls). You
order the Rancher's Flat
Iron Steak. It's 1:38. The
waitress isn't what you'd
expect. Nice enough. No
attitude. Not too

much of anything.
There's a kid busing
tables. He's got problems.
His apron is untied.
A guy in a suit calls
him a *waterheaded*

jackoff when he bumps
him with the gray plastic tub
he's carrying on his hip.
The man behind you
tells a woman that she
must *be honest above all else.*
She doesn't say

anything. Her phone rings.
He whispers. The waitress comes.
The woman orders a steak:
A big, thick one she says loud.
He can't eat at a time
like this. You eye

the candy rack for
a Cherry Mash
or a Moon Pie. A guy
wearing a seed corn cap
and plaid

sleeves has his face buried
in a laptop. He stands.
Reaches for a book
and tells the woman
at the register if anyone
needs him, he'll be

(no stanza break)

in the library. She doesn't
look up from the ticket she's
figuring. An Amish couple
wait. Young. He barely

has a beard. It's 2:01.
You guess he only takes
her out this late
to avoid the stares.
You try not to

look as you head
for the john.
You see his boots
and the book under the stall.
There's a bloody handprint

on the cover. It's called
Killing Floor. He whistles.
You cough. Drop a quarter
in the slot.

Twist the knob.

Rough Traces

The fuckers that fly
fancy themselves
over us. With their
costly rods and ties.
They wouldn't stoop
to cat. And plumb
sure wouldn't roll
dough and cast from
a brown river's edge.

I nod and say
Fuckin' A.

I reach for a liver.
Slide it on a three
aught Eagle Claw
and make a careful
cast past our lantern.
I lay my gerry-rigged
Johnson in a Cotton-
wood fork.

Sit with my arms
around my knees
So still the pulse
begins to rock me.

Their pretty fish. Hip
waders. Baskets and
nets. The whole damn
affair. Like Brad Pitt
in that shitty flick.

It ain't no way to fish.

I shake my head and
sip a Mickey's. I don't
say more than I do.
Like that I just finished
a book by Hemingway.
That I want to read him
how Jake caught trout.
How he dressed them
out and packed them
in a basket with ferns.
How he cooled two

bottles of wine in
a stream. How he
slept waiting for
Bill to finish with
his fly rod resting.
in its case.

But where to begin?
A book. Europe. And
trout. So. Instead
of trying, I give.

I reach for the stringer
and pull up six
barking cats. Four
Channel. Two Blues.

He says *it's a fine
mess* and I say Yep.

I gill the big one
then make him quiver
with a rock. He shines
in the kerosene light.
I nail his head to a tree,
grab the needle nose
and strip the skin. Take
a knife and gut him.
I toss the tangle away.

He wonders *if it could
be bait.* Sure thing, I say.

I make two fillets. Pack
them in newspaper
and lay then in the
styrofoam cooler he
brought the Mickey's in.

He says *why.*
I say never mind.

I go on with the others.
Get horned once. He
says to *rub the stuck
spot on the cat's belly
to heal it right up.*

Right, I say.

I don't hear them
bark anymore. I smack
their heads on rocks
and watch them flip
and die. I swing the hammer
and let them fall in a pile.
I slice them into strips
and pack them away.

I wash the dough and
liver, the slime and
blood from my hands
in the river. I have
the last Mickey's
and lay back thinking
about what he said.
What I'd like to say.
About my rough
traces and about Jake.

HHII III

Better Men Than You

when it happens

you try to explain
what makes
you keep at it.
why you work
this much
of yourself into it.
how you can turn it over
and over again
in your head.
how it's held
together.
how it all moves,
you say, explaining.
the works
of it.
see?
how it's done
in better men
than you.
that it leaves you
awake after
strange hunches,
shifting inclinations,
subtle ramifications
and
and you notice
your dark hands, reaching
like a tent-revival preacher's
and you look over
sure
she hasn't heard
a word
of it
and part of you is glad
she can sleep
at a time like this.

Cover Image:
Shawnee Cycle Company (Topeka, KS), 1913. Courtesy of the
Kansas State Historical Society.
Image FK2.S5/T.73/M.SHA/*1

Epigraph:
Found on page xxvi of the Foreword to A. E. Hotchner's *Papa
Hemingway* (1999: Carroll & Graf Publishers, Inc.)

The Flea Market In White Cloud:
White Cloud, a town of about 200, is off K-7 in Doniphan
County, KS. Each Memorial and Labor Day a large flea mar-
ket is held that attracts visitors from several states.

She Says Timothy:
Timothy is a grass used for cattle feed and horse hay. It was
named for an American farmer, Timothy Hanson, that promot-
ed its cultivation in the early/mid 18th Century.

The Jackfruit Tree:
The Jackfruit Tree is indigenous to west India, but can also be
found in Southeast Asia, Africa, The Philippines and Brasil.
Jackfruit is the largest tree-borne fruit in the world, reaching up
to 80 pounds in weight, 36 inches in length and 20 inches in
diameter.

Salamonie:
The Salamonie is a 2,665 acre reservoir in the Indiana counties
of Wabash and Huntington.

Sometimes I Take My Bike:
Jack Kerouac is to have said "Anyone can make Paris holy, but
I can make Topeka holy."

Kentucky Bottoms:
Kentucky Bottoms was an early name for the town of Perry,
KS. It was apt as the town is located in Kentucky Township
and is in the Kansas River bottom lands. The town was formal-
ly incorporated as Perry after the President of the Union Pacific
Railroad.

Keats:
Keats is a small town in Riley County, KS. Latitude 39.223N.
Longitude 96.708W. The poet mentioned is B.H. Fairchild.
The poem is his "Keats" which can be found in his fine collec-
tion *The Art of the Lathe* (1998: Alice James Books).

Letter from Muscotah:
From a letter written by Eric Heineken on October 11, 2001 as
part of the Day in My Community Project.

Grissom A. F. B.:
Grissom Air Force Base is located in Miami County, IN. In the
early 80's it was rumored to have been on the first strike list of
the U. S. S. R. It was named for Virgil "Gus" Grissom, an
Indiana astronaut, who died January 27, 1967 in the Appollo
204 fire at Cape Kennedy.

Roscoe Fearing Falters:
Kenneth Fearing was a poet and novelist in early/mid twentieth
century New York. This poem is a riff on his "Jack Knuckles
Falters" that can be found in *Complete Poems* (1994: The
National Poetry Foundation) among other places.

city-broke:
The title was taken from the Carl Sandberg poem "[Wilderness
Man]" in which includes the lines "But why did he rush along
like a city-broke / newspaper delivery horse." The poem is
included in *Poems for the People* (1999: Ivan R. Dee).

Kingdom Farm:
Kingdom Farm was a utopian community founded near
Manhattan, KS by Wilhelm Hoade. It lasted for several years,
even past Hoade's death in 1852, eventually disbanding about
1859. See *The Hoadite Community at Kingdom Farm* by Paul
Kettle (1958: Kansas State Univ. Press). A poetic treatment is
John Wood's *The Gates of the Elect Kingdom* (1997: Univ. of Iowa
Press).

Rough Traces:
The book mentioned is *The Sun Also Rises*

Acknowledgements

The Argo: "Delilah Shopteese and Her Pug Ruckus,"
"For Some Years the Janitor at Lowman"

Chiron Review: "city-broke"

Circle Magazine: "The Flea Market in White Cloud"

Coal City Review: "One Man's Junk," "Terminal"

The Dead Mule: "Muscadine," "Cheat River Coffinworks"

Flint Hills Review: "The Jackfruit Tree," "Valley Falls"

Kansas City Star: "Gorgeous George's Used Hat Emporium"

Lawrence Journal-World: "Perry," "when it happens"

Mind0: "Pennsylvania"

Present Magazine: "A Clean Seam," "not too good," "Revival
Antiques"

Pulsar Poetry Magazine: "Jack at the Jetlag"

Red River Review: "Stillwater"

The Same: "Flush or Bust"

Skidrow Penthouse: "Kentucky Bottoms"

Whistling Shade: "She Says Timothy"

Some of these poems also appeared in an untitled chapbook,
Prospero's Pocket Poets, Volume 2, Number 2 (Unholy Day Press
and Blue Cow Press, 2004)

Thanks

To: You for giving this a read.

To: The Management for putting this show on the road.

To: Christine Ewing for the design.

To: Cat for the photogs.

To: Joseph Isahack for the flash art. www. josephisahack.com

To: All the patient folks that read various drafts of the
manuscript, especially:
Philip Heldrich, Gary Lechliter, Sarah Ruhlen,
Lou Ann Thomas and Mary Wharff.

To: The community of poets in and around Lawrence, KS.

To: O. P. G. for not having by-laws, a secret handshake or rules
of order. Reprobates. The lot of ya.

To: Jennifer.

Jason Wesco's great^5-grandfather, John Henry, died in Riley County, Kansas Territory on March 19, 1856. He had in his possession at the time of his death: a trunk; a few suits of clothes; a German Bible; a pocket watch; and a copy of his will. He is thought to have arrived by steamship with a party that originated from Cincinnati. The cause of his death is unknown, though he was aged 76 years, 10 months and 23 days and had buried two wives, Margaret and Ann. John Henry's father and grand-father, Matthias and Francois, both served in the 1st Company, Northampton County (PA) Militia during the Revolutionary War. His great-grandfather, Jean Philippe Vesqueau, a Huguenot refugee from the Alsace region of France (between the Rhine River and Vosges Mountains), arrived at the Port of Philadelphia in 1754 aboard the ship *Phoenix*. John Henry was a farmer. He signed his name as X. It is not known why he came to Kansas.

John Henry's great^5-grandson has spent the last ten years of his life in Kansas. He now lives in Pittsburg, KS and can be reached at: zeke@219press.com.